MW01120042

THE GREATEST PUPPET SHOW ON EARTH

Charlene Anderson

Beacon Hill Press of Kansas City
Kansas City, Missouri

Contents

CHAPTER 1

Peter's Idea

Peter Jose Morgan was in third grade. The first four grades at school were watching a puppet show. A first grader played the part of Neddy Nutrient. Peter thought he was awful. How was anyone going to learn about eating right from him?

Peter turned around. Two rows back, his friend Bunde was holding his nose. Peter smiled and nodded in agreement.

Nathan Nixon, the fourth grade bully, began to holler: "Boo! Boo! Bad acting."

The director came out from behind the stage. "That concludes the first graders' part of the show. I will finish the play."

Mr. Robinson put the Neddy puppet on his hand and went behind the stage. Peter

called to him, "Hey, Neddy! What should I have for lunch today?"

"A hot dog and french fries," cried Neddy in a squeaky voice. Everyone laughed. Mr. Robinson was funny.

"Not hot dogs," shouted Nathan. "They're too greasy."

"Not hot dogs," cried the first graders sitting on the floor.

Mama Puppet scolded, "Shame on you, Neddy Nutrient. It's not right to trick these children into eating greasy foods."

Something whizzed past Peter's nose—a spit wad. He looked at Bunde. Bunde pointed to Nathan. Peter turned and made a face at Nathan. Nathan made one back.

Peter turned back to the puppet show. "Phooey! I'll never get a hot dog on this show," wailed Neddy. "Can I have Cheerios instead?"

"Oh yes," said Mama Puppet. "Oats are very nutritious. How did you ever think of that?"

"I'm schmart—very schmart," answered Neddy.

"Boys and girls, you, too, can be smart. Make sure you eat right every day. Good-bye," called Neddy. Then he dropped out of sight.

CHAPTER 2

Peter's Puppet Show

Back in class, Miss Trumpet said, "We're having free time now. Each person can build whatever he or she likes out of this pile of cardboard."

Peter had a terrific idea. He'd make his own puppet stage and puppets. He got some construction paper, tape, foam balls, and other supplies. He taped, stapled, glued, and cut. But Peter couldn't make his stage stand up. Bunde was busy, so Peter asked Jamie Gomez to help him. Jamie's folks had moved here from some place called Cuba.

When Miss Trumpet called on Peter to show his project, Peter bowed low. "Ta-dah," he said. Then he ducked down and held up his puppet. Jamie held the stage. Peter's puppet had a round Styrofoam head, yellow yarn hair, and black paper eyes.

"I am Neddy Nutrient," he said in a funny voice.

"Did everyone have breakfast today?" Some kids shouted yes. Some said no.

"You must always eat breakfast. Breakfast gives you brainpower. You need brainpower to do your schoolwork." Peter finished and stood up.

"Bring back Neddy Nutrient," shouted the third graders.

Miss Trumpet smiled. "Great idea, Peter. Now, why did you make a puppet stage and puppet?"

"I want to be a teacher like Mr. Robinson," he said. "It's important that everyone eat the right foods. They need to be healthy."

"We never eat right," said Jamie. "Maybe that's why I'm sick so much. We don't have a regular house either. Sometimes we even have cardboard walls." Everyone turned and stared at him.

Peter felt sorry for him. He knew how shy Jamie was. Thinking fast, he said, "Maybe I could bring a puppet show about eating right out to where you live?"

"*Sí*" (pronounced SEE; *sí* means "yes" in Spanish), said Jamie. "Maybe you could."

CHAPTER 3

Peter's First Show

Peter and Bunde talked to Jamie about taking a puppet show to the migrant camp.

"*Sí, sí!*" said Jamie, grinning from ear to ear.

"I have to get home," said Bunde as he headed for his bike.

"I'm walking," said Peter. "I have to carry my puppet stage. See you both tomorrow."

When Peter got home, he yelled for his mother.

"Mom! Come and see what I made at school!"

"I can't now," she cried from the kitchen. "Bring it in here."

Peter pushed open the kitchen door. "What's going on?"

"I'm making dinner. Why don't you set the table and tell me about what you made. Set an extra place too. Grandma is coming."

During dinner, Grandma did all of the talking. She was thrilled with her new senior center. "All kinds of events are planned," she said. "We even have a doctor. He doesn't charge us anything.

"Also, we are to take a food item every time we go to the center. The food will be given to help people who are hungry. The director hasn't decided where yet."

After dinner, Peter called Bunde. Bunde came over and brought his puppets. They put on a puppet show for the family.

Peter held up his puppet first.

In a squeaky voice he said, "Hi, folks. My name is Neddy Nutrient."

Bunde turned his puppet toward the audience. "And my name is Tony Sweet Tooth. We are glad you are here."

The boys finished their program, and Father called out, "Good job, boys."

"Do you think we're good enough to do puppet shows for real people?" asked Peter.

"I think so," said Father. "By the way, we're real people."

Peter grinned and nodded.

"Where did you want to give your puppet show?" asked Mother.

"At migrant camp," said Peter.

"Not a good idea," said Mother.

"Why not?"

"Those people live on the other side of the tracks," said Mother.

"There are no tracks in this town," complained Peter.

"Your mother means they're a different class," said Father.

"Then I'm in a different class, too, aren't I? Didn't the adoption people tell you I was born in South America?"

"That's enough, Peter Jose," said Father.

CHAPTER 4

Peter Gets Help

Peter passed Nathan's house the next day on the way to school. He heard Nathan's mother and father hollering at each other. A few seconds later, Nathan rushed out the front door and jumped on his bike.

Peter felt sick when Nathan headed toward him. The next minute, Nathan was ramming his bike into Peter's bike.

"Cut it out!" shouted Peter, jerking his bike away.

"Ha, ha, ha," laughed Nathan. "I showed you. My new bike is better than yours any day."

"Look at my fender. You've wrecked it," cried Peter, doubling up a fist.

Nathan laughed again. "What do you think you're going to do with that fist?" Then he turned and rode away.

"Now I know what Daniel felt like in the lions' den," Peter muttered.

At school, Bunde helped Peter straighten his fender. While they worked, Jamie Gomez walked up. "Everyone at our place thinks the puppet show is a great idea," he said.

"We can't come," said Peter.

Jamie's face fell. "My mama didn't think you would." The bell rang for school to start. The boys went to class.

Peter felt bad because the other boys and girls made fun of Jamie.

"Jamie's dirty. Look at his hands!"

"Yeah, and my dad says his family is shifty."

"What does that mean?"

"They're dishonest. And they go from place to place. They change jobs all the time."

"Jamie's not dirty," said Peter. "And who says he's dishonest? Stop talking about him like that."

After school, Peter went to Miss Trumpet. "Miss Trumpet, would you go to migrant camp with Bunde and me? We want to take our puppet show there."

"I think that's possible," said Miss Trumpet.

"Maybe my parents will let me go if you go too," said Peter.

"My grandma says the senior center is collecting food for hungry people. Maybe the director would let us take that too. Jamie says he doesn't eat right. He thinks maybe that's why he's sick so much."

"It could be," said Miss Trumpet.

CHAPTER 5

Double Trouble

On the way to church the next morning Peter was really happy. His parents agreed he could go to the migrant camp if his teacher went with them.

Peter's Sunday School teacher was sick, so he went upstairs to the teen class with Tom, the pastor's son. Peter liked Tom, and he'd been to the teen class before. But he didn't always understand what they were talking about. His mind wandered.

But when the teacher said, "Lots of people you know are hungry and poor," Peter snapped to attention. Grandma had said almost the same thing. He didn't know anyone who might be hungry except maybe Jamie.

"Many people who don't look hungry really are. Sometimes they are hungry for someone to speak a kind word to them. Sometimes just a smile is all they need."

"Where does it say all that in the Bible?" asked Peter.

"Matthew 25:35, 'For I was hungry and you gave me something to eat,'" said the teacher.

"Hmmm," thought Peter.

Peter knew Bunde was waiting for him to get home from church. He wanted to work with their puppets again. When Peter got home, he called Bunde to come over.

The side door to the garage was open when the boys got there. "This door wasn't open when we left to go to church," said Peter. He stepped inside and felt sick. Someone had torn up his cardboard stage.

"What a mess," cried Bunde.

"Mother! Dad!" yelled Peter at the top of his lungs.

Peter's mother and father came running. Father pushed open the garage door as Nathan rode up on his bike.

"What happened?" asked Nathan, looking around.

Peter pointed to the broken stage. His bushy hair and angry eyes made him look fierce. "As if you didn't know, Nathan Nixon! You did it, didn't you?"

"No, no, it wasn't me!" cried the fourth grader.

CHAPTER 6

Miss Trumpet Gets the Mumps

On Monday, Peter and Bunde told Miss Trumpet about the wrecked stage.

"Oh, that's awful," she said. "Now don't wait too long to build a new one. The pickers will be moving on very soon."

Jamie had said the puppet show should be in the evening. That's when the pickers got home from the fields. Peter and Bunde planned a Friday night when Miss Trumpet could go with them.

Bunde's father was a doctor and good with his hands. He helped the boys make another stage out of plywood. Bunde's mother made a red-and-white-striped curtain. The boys hurried to Bunde's basement every day after school to fix the new stage. Every day Nathan asked Peter to let him help too.

"Stay away," sneered Peter. "You're not going to ruin another stage for us."

One day while they were working in the basement, Bunde's mom came downstairs with a box.

"A package for Peter," she said.

"Who would be sending me a package?" he asked.

Peter ripped open the box. "Look!" he cried. "Puppets! Real puppets."

"Whoopee!" cried Bunde.

"We are going to have the greatest puppet show in the whole world!" shouted Peter.

The night before the show Peter couldn't sleep. He got up earlier than usual. As he was eating breakfast, the phone rang.

"Good morning," he answered happily.

"This is Miss Trumpet," said the voice at the other end of the line. "I'm sorry. I can't go to migrant camp with you tonight. I have the mumps."

"Oh no," groaned Peter. He was so upset, he hung up without even saying good-bye. He didn't want to tell his mother about Miss Trumpet. He was afraid she would say he couldn't go. He opened the back door and headed for school.

His mother called out the door after him, "You haven't eaten breakfast."

"I'm not hungry. I've got to see Bunde."

"You need brainpower to be schmart, really schmart, remember?"

Peter remembered and went back to eat breakfast. He was glad she hadn't asked about the phone call.

Jamie rode up to Peter as soon as he got to school. "Everything's set for tonight," he said. "We can't wait."

Peter couldn't tell Jamie Miss Trumpet was sick. It was too awful.

When the bell rang for class to start, the principal walked into the classroom. "I am your teacher this morning," he said. "Miss Trumpet is sick."

Jamie's mouth dropped open. He looked at Peter. Peter knew he had hurt Jamie's feelings. He should have told him about Miss Trumpet.

CHAPTER 7

Peter Finds a Way

At recess, Peter found Jamie.

"Don't worry," said Peter. "Bunde and I will be there."

Peter had just thought of someone who might go with them. He had to act fast. As soon as school was out, he rode off on his bike to find Tom, the pastor's son. Tom ran every afternoon on the high school track. When Peter got there, Tom was putting on his track shoes.

"Hi, Tom," he waved.

"Good to see you, buddy," said Tom. "You gonna run with me?"

"No," said Peter.

"What's up, then?" asked Tom.

The words spilled out of Peter, like water gushing from a fountain. "Remember I told you about the puppet show and Miss Trumpet?"

"Sure do," said Tom.

"Our show is tonight, and everyone is expecting us. But Miss Trumpet is sick. Will you go with us?"

"Peter, I'd really like to, but I promised Nathan we'd do something together."

"Oh . . . Nathan . . ."

"Nathan's my buddy," Tom explained. "But I'll see if he wants to do something tomorrow instead."

"He's a big bully," said Peter. "He won't want to help. He ruins everything."

"Well, let's ask him. He'll be here in a minute."

Just then Nathan came running up.

"Peter's got a problem, old buddy," said Tom. "He wants us to help him out."

"Us?" Peter thought. "Oh no! He's inviting Nathan to come!"

Tom explained everything to Nathan.

"Sure, I'll come," said Nathan.

"Peter, it's a deal," said Tom. "We'll pick you up at seven."

"Thank you! Thank you," cried Peter.

"Nathan, if you and Peter are going to work together, you'd better shake on it."

Peter held out his hand. Nathan just stood there.

"Come on, Nathan," urged Tom. "Tell him!"

"I did it," admitted Nathan. "I wrecked your stage."

"I knew it!" yelled Peter.

"I'm sorry," Nathan went on. "That's why I wanted to help you build a new stage. Did you get my package?"

"Package?" asked Peter. "What package?"

"The puppets."

"You're the one who sent the puppets?" Peter couldn't believe his ears.

The Migrant Camp
Puppet Show

Tom and Nathan picked up Peter and Bunde and their stage. Then they picked up four boxes of food from the senior center. Peter couldn't wait to see Jamie's face when he saw all the food.

The migrant camp ran alongside the berry fields, winding up and down the hillside. Soon they came to a row of small shacks.

"There's Jamie," cried Nathan. "Hi, Jamie," he yelled, jumping out of the car.

"Nathan! I didn't know you were coming," said Jamie.

"He's the one who sent us the new puppets," said Peter.

"Wow," said Jamie. Then he said, "Come on. I want to show you where I live." Jamie walked to the shack closest to the road. A single lightbulb hung on a wire in the middle of the room. Three beds lined the wall. A little girl lay asleep on one of the beds, sucking her thumb.

"That's my little sister," said Jamie. "She works in the fields too. Mama let her come home early because of the puppet show."

"I thought you had cardboard walls," said Nathan.

"We do at some towns. Not here. We even have a bathroom."

"You mean you don't always have a bathroom?" said Nathan. "That's awful."

"It's hard when you're sick," said Jamie.

None of the cupboards had doors. It was easy to see there wasn't much food. The food from the senior center was going to help a lot.

One of the children called to Peter. Suddenly, he realized the others were setting up the puppet stage without him.

Boys, girls, mothers, and fathers sat on the ground. Some sat on the hoods of trucks and upside-down pails. Others leaned against trees.

"Everyone's here except my mama and papa," said Jamie. "We must wait."

"Can we sit with Jamie and his mama and papa when they get here, Tom?" asked Nathan.

"You go ahead," said Tom. "I won't be sitting much. I'll be busy taking pictures."

Just then a car drove up. It was Bunde's father. "Dad, what are you doing here?" cried Bunde. "I didn't know you were coming."

Bunde's father winked at Peter. "Peter asked me to come," he said. He got out his black bag and put his stethoscope around his neck.

"We're waiting for Jamie's mama and papa before we start the show," said Peter. "Do whatever you can."

"Hello, young one," said the doctor to Jamie's little sister, who was pulling on her right ear. "Is that ear bothering you?"

The little girl looked down. Jamie put his arm around her. "It's OK, Maria. The nice man wants to help you. Didn't you tell me your ear hurt?"

"Uh-huh," said Maria, looking up.

"Maybe this man can help you."

Maria stepped toward Bunde's father. He talked to her awhile. Then he went to see other children. Soon Jamie's mama and papa drove up in an old red Ford pickup.

It was almost dark when they got there. Mr. Gomez had all the cars and trucks turn on their headlights to light up the puppet stage.

Peter and Bunde gave their show. Everyone laughed and sang and had a good time. Tom got pictures of everything.

Soon the show was over. "That's all, folks, except one more surprise," said Peter in his booming puppet voice.

"Look over here." He pointed to the food from the senior center.

"We brought you a gift from the seniors in town," he said. "Their gift will help you eat right, just as we've been talking about in our show. Take whatever you need."

Most of the adults went to the food boxes. Many hadn't eaten all day except for berries picked in the fields.

Jamie went to Peter and just stood there. Very quietly he said, "Peter, my friend, thank you."

The children crowded around the puppet stage, crying, "Stay." "Give us another show," they cheered.

Nathan jumped up. He got his puppet out of his backpack and told the children to follow him.

"What's he up to?" asked Peter, watching them go.

"He's up to no good, I'll bet," said Bunde. But Nathan surprised them both. He put on his own puppet show for the children.

"I've never seen Nathan happy before," said Peter. "I guess Tom's right. He's not such a bully after all."

Bunde's father gave shots and medicine to as many people as needed them.

Peter had fun making the children laugh and sing. And he was glad he'd thought to bring food. Maybe now Jamie would feel better.

After a while, Tom called out, "Time to go."

On the way home, Peter and Nathan rode with Tom, and Bunde rode with his father.

"Nathan," said Peter. "You wrecked my fender and called me names. Now you're acting nice. Why?"

"I don't know if I should tell you. Promise you won't tell—not even Bunde?"

"I promise," said Peter.

"My mom and dad have been meeting with the pastor. Tom has been working with me. I understand a little better why my dad acts so mean."

Peter listened. Then he answered, "Hey, I have an idea. Would you help Bunde and me give our puppet shows from now on?"

"You mean it? Sure!" said Nathan. It was dark in the car, but Peter could see Nathan was smiling. He felt good inside because Nathan looked happy. Peter remembered the words of the teen teacher, "Often just a kind word or a smile is all that is necessary."